KNOCK KNOCK JOKES FOR KIDS:

LOUGH OUT LOUD JOKES

MIKE FERRIS

Why are some words in books longer than others?

Because they tell the author 'letters in!'

Captain Kirk wrecked my chair

Starring William Satinher

My geography teacher is so rubbish he told me to get lost.

And I did

Who is the cinema married to?

The cineda

What's further away than a safari?

A toofari.

Why have elephants got big ears?

Because Noddy won't pay the ransom.

Knock knock

Who's there?

Han sole

Han sole who?

Tell Jabba I'll have his money.

Riding bikes without handlebars

By Lindsay Nohands

What do blue bottle stunt pilots fly?

Loop da poop.

My friends and I sing together, and stick together. We're in the Glue club.

Why did the Chicken flap so much Because he had some hotwings'

Waiter this eggs too hardboiled.

How can an egg be too hard boiled?

It just joined the police.

I've got a pirate car.

Is it fuel efficient?

It gets 100 miles per galleon.

The coach must be enormous, if he can carry the whole football team to the game!

We just bought a German Shepherd dog. It should come in handy if we need to round up any Germans.

Q. What does a duck put in its soup?

A. Quackers!

My dad's so stupid, when the computer got a virus he poured chicken soup into the keyboard.

What do monsters call Halloween?

Dress down Thursday.

Mr and Mrs Fishent and their unreliable son Ian.

Why are bees so famous? There's always a buzz about them

My cat loves rap music so much, I've bought him his own scratching post.

How does a DVD get exercise?

By skipping

Why did the dinner lady always serve the same type of potato?

She had no imashination

How did the coat feel like it was giving the wearer a hug?

It was a coat of arms

What do you call an angry stamp collector?

A stomp collector

Son when I was your age; we had to walk 10 miles to school and 10 miles back again. Didn't matter if it was raining or snowing. And it taught me one important lesson.

What lesson was that dad?

Where the school bus stop was.

Q. Why did the snake take a job biting its own tail?

A. It was trying to make ends meet.

What's the dullest part of a computer?

The keybored

What does a detective take on a picnic?

A hunch-box

Why is salmon messy? Because you always get salmon you.

Knock knock

Who's there?

Yah

Yah Who?

Yeeha!

What kind of German car is also a puppet?

An Audi Doody.

I've got lucky sporting socks, they've got a hole in one.

Where do cavemen fly on a plane?

Club class.

I wanted to ride horses at the circus but they wanted me to jump through too many hoops.

When's the best time to trade insults? At the end of term dissco

The bags on plane story

With Jim Carryon Luggage.

Mr and Mrs Foot and their clumsy son Emanuel Cortez

I'm taking my mum to the capital of Indonesia?

Jakarta

No we're taking the bus.

I got arrested for putting cheese too high in the fridge.

They thought I was a high way man.

Which Swedish band can't keep a secret?

BLABBA

Q. How do cats show they like something?

A. Give it a round of a-paws!

Waiter what's in this pie?

Lungs, liver and stomach sir.

It's offal!

What's the best site for gossip?

Two face book.

What do Shakespeare say when he was thinking about buying a cat? "tabby or not tabby?"

Knock Knock

Who's there?

Dan

Dan who?

Down here, I'm very short!

Did you hear about the edible book?

It was b-read

Did you hear about the hat that was three styles in one?

It was a hat-trick

My Mum told me to do some home-work…

So I washed the windows

What sort of jacket is worn to play outside?

A parka

The good news is you can stay up all night watching a horror film

The bad news is the film is your parents wedding video

How do you get the attention of the end of a skirt?

Say 'a-hem'

What does a king like best in his pencil case?

The ruler

What do you call a song by an ill singer?

Musick

How to be a tyrant by Dick Tater

The good news is I remembered to bring my home work into school

The badnews is I forgot it's Saturday

What do you call a dish of uncooked beef? Not roast.

Dad you're so old when you went to school there were only 6
stars on the

flag.

Know your own mind by May Dupp

Knock knock

Who's there?

Sh

Shwho?

Well hurry up and drop the other one

We were learning about fairy tales today.

Snow white? Cinderella?

Political studies.

Why can you hear a doorbell?

Because of bellectricity

What do you call a group made up of the kids of musicians?

Heir-band

Introduction to astronomy by Stella View

What's Australia's favourite candy? W&Ws

When I was your age I got fit and earned money delivering papers

You must have dad they were on stone tablets back then

Knock knock

Who's there?

Day

Day who?

Daylight come and me wanna go home!

Daddy I got 5 out of 5 at school today.

Well done son.

I got an E from all 5 teachers.

Waiter try this soup.

What's wrong with it?

How am I supposed to study the founding fathers when none of them had a blog?

Where do vampires go when they sleep?

Dracu la la land.

Drunken movie

With Sharon Stoned

Q. How to trees get into facebook?

A. They log in.

How do footballers send letters?

Through the goalpost

Where does baby fruit sleep?

In the apri-cot

What did the shoe say when the other shoe was talking too much?

Put a sock in it

Why can't desks face the other way?

Because sksed isn't a word

What do you use to make art quickly?

A paint-rush

The good news is you've got the biggest part in the school play

The bad news is your playing the back end of an elephant

Whats a gangsters favourite food? A pizza the action.

Where would you like the mac and cheese sir?

Over my head.

But why sir?

It's raining outside.

Why do zombies make good plumbers?

They know everything about, draaaaaaains!

How to make wine

With Danny Devino

The donkey movie

With Daniel Bray Lewis

Mr and Mrs Tickles and their short sighted son Spec

How do you go on the holiday of your dreams?

Sleep on the plane.

What do vampires rob?

Blood banks.

Which bands annoy people on the internet? Rock and Troll bands.

Why did the football coach keep taking the rival teams coke bottles to the store?

He wanted their quarter back.

I'm so scared of flying I don't use runways.

I use runaways.

What's the laziest item in the playground? The kipping rope

Knock Knock

Who's there?

Shirley

Shirley who?

Surely you recognise me by now

Q. Where do vampires buy their art supplies?

A. Pencil-vania.

What's the meanest food?

Rude-barb

What do feet most love to dance to?

A socksophone

Why is science sometimes difficult?

Because of the chemystery

Teacher: Which element has the Chemical symbol Zn

Franz: Um...errrr

Teacher: Zinc!

Franz: I am Zinking!

The good news is an art school wants to use you as a model

The bad news is they're painting furniture

I steal baby goats when they're asleep

I'm a kidnapper

Why are open top cars ambitious?

Because they're roofless.

What's the friendliest Olympic sport?

The Hi Jump!

So the stewardess asks everyone; "can you fly a plane?"

Are we crashing?

No I need a date and I've got high standards.

You can't get a pay raise working for the circus.

Event the elephants work for peanuts.

Teacher: Can you name a Nursery Rhyme?

Julie: Bursary!

My brothers so stupid, he brought a lawn mower to school so he could cut class.

Why are bees so successful in the army? They always earn their stripes

I tried to follow my pet Cat wherever he went. But I ended up getting in a

flap about it.

Knock Knock

Who's there?

Terry

Terry who?

Terrible weather out here, hurry up!

Q. Why did the millionaire quit her job as a baker?

A. Because she didn't kneed the dough!

What game can you play when you've got a cold?

Statchoos

How did the butter knife get stuck?

It was in a jam

What did the left hand say to the right hand when they played in the snow?

'This is so glovely'

Where do explorers learn how to eat well?

In Captain Cook-ery class

I'm so unpopular my imaginary friend defriended me.

Who haunts your nose?

The booger man.

What do; witches and mad axe men have for breakfast?

Snap, cackle and chop,

The newspaper man

Starring Kurt Russell

Mr and Mrs Cheese and their son Mac

What music camp is forbidden?

Band camp

Q. What part of the kitchen is best at math?

A. The counter.

Why was the monkey drunk?

He'd been at the monkey bars

What did the potato say to his son?

'You're a chip off the old block'

Where do you keep old maths books?

In mathem-attics

Q. Fly did the building float away?

A. It was a light house.

How to run for ages by Mary Thon

The good news is there are no rats in the school canteen

The bad news is because the rats ate them

What kind of candy is past it's sell by date? Jelly hasbeans

Son I was at school things weren't so easy. At recess we had to chase the monkeys off the monkey bars.

How to empty a bath by Paula plug

Knock knock

Who's there?

Pill

Pill who?

It's too early for bed

Q. What did the ref say to the cheating turkey?

A. FOWL!

How did the naughty puddle introduce itself?

'My name's mud'

Which food is hardest to find?

Spagyeti

What is kept in Willie Wonka's wardrobe?

Joompah-loompahs

When I was your age we had to make our own entertainment

Yeh but you had diplodocuses to slide off of dad

Which Sesame street character should I mug by, Robert (Rob Bert)

The maths teacher said we'd have to buy protractors for class. What's his angle?

Knock knock

Who's there?

Amish

Amish who?

I'm right here!

Who was the first rock band?

The rolling flint stones.

What did Dracula say when he bit the truck.

A van to bite your neck.

I hate watching people jump off of boards, they're always taking dives.

Why do lumberjacks make good helicopter pilots?

They know how to handle a chopper.

The whole second half of the show is clowns throwing custard flans at each other.

It's a pie lot project.

They told me I could be the chairman of the circus.

In the lion's cage.

What happened when you got an F in art class son?

The teacher opened the window.

Q.   How does a snake get into Hogwarts

A.   Slitherin

What kind of sauce is this?

It's the number one source of diarrhoea

Look how well I'm doing at Latin dad!

Son it says how often you've been late in!

What's the happiest kind of cat? A purrrssssian

Q. Why do cats take so long to sign a contract?

A. They like to read every claws.

Why do clocks like apples?

Because of the pips

How did the silly boy try to connect his TV and DVD player?

A scarf-lead

What was the tree told when it wore antique jewellery?

'You can tell a tree's age by its rings'

What do you call a collection of jokes?

A Lollection

How to speak French by Harley Francais

The good news is we won't be doing dodge ball in gym today

The bad news is the balls still there you're just not allowed to dodge it

Why won't dad share his snacks at the cinema? Because it's pop's corn.

When I was your age we were so broke all I had for lunch was a sandwich of two slices of bread and hope for filling.

Bathrooms next to bedrooms by Ron Suite

Knock knock

Who's there?

Twittwa

Twitwawho?

You still got those darn owls!

I went camping with school.

Was it exciting?

It was in tents.

This meal is like a fine work of art waiter.

Is it that beautiful sir?

No I can't afford to pay for it.

Why wouldn't the ghost make her bed?

She was a bansheet.

Q. Why did the pepper go to prison?

A. A Salt

One of my sons is plump

With Robert Fatterson

Mr and Mrs Kell and their well preserved daughter Pick.

I'm going on an economic wood work camp

It's awl included in the price.

Some body stole my Christmas Marzipan cake.

It was stohlen.

What award do old rockers get?

The Grammies.

Q. What's a sheep's favorite food?

A. BaaaaaaaBeQue

What did the confused fireman wear?

A blaze-er

How to fry anything by Chris Pee

The good news is somebody sent you a valentine's card

The bad news is its your teacher.

How to rob banks by Hans Up

The good news is your in the school's model UN

The bad news is you're in detention for being a war criminal

Want's the most stubborn cake? A muffin doin'

The most unpopular man in the world

Starring Sylvester Alone.

I went on a biking holiday in Australia.

We rode down route 99.

The mafia have banned their members from using twitter, in case they tweet like canaries.

Why are all cars fat?
Because they've got a trunk with a spare tyre.

What position do convicts play in football? They're always in goal.

What channel do pirates take through airport customs?
Booty free.

Have you heard of the new dragon based circus?
Burn 'em and Bailey.

Why was the boy's bag so heavy? He'd accidentally picked up his rocksack

What's the most beautiful part of school? The school-belle

Why can't you teach Cowboys Art?

Because if you ask them to draw they'll fire a gun

I've got myself a Lizard.... Lizard.... Lizard. Hang on, I think there's a 'Gecko' in here.

Knock Knock. Who's there?

Woo.

Woo Who!

At last someone is pleased to see me

Q. Who are the warmest competitors at the Olympics?

A. The long jumpers.

What's a wasp's favourite sport?

Rugbee

What's the quickest dessert?

Race-pudding

No-one could win the terrible game of tug-rope…

It was a tie

How to put on an opera by Des Valkyrie

The good news is I came second in my race in school

The news is the bully came first

Why do sea captains make great pilots?

Because it's plane sailing.

The circus is going broke. They just fired the human cannon ball!

Why can't you protest at school? Because they've got marching band.

I want to study a dead language

Latin?

Zombie eeuuurrrgggh

I went to a nomad school last year

Was it tough?

It was in tents.

Q. What's a baker's favorite movie?

A. Pie School Musical

What happens after we all fall down in ring o'roses?

Ring a'rises

What's a musicians favourite sweet?

Humbugs

What do you call an artist who lives in a cupboard?

A drawer

Knock knock

Who's there?

Sool

Sool who?

Shouldn't you be on the Enterprise?

Q. Why did the grizzly have no friends?

A. He was unbearable.

Back when I was at school we had respect for our teachers

I can respect them for putting up with you.

Just try it.

What's wrong with it?

Just try it.

There's no spoon.

Exactly.

What's a ghosts favourite website?

Yahboo!

What do Australian ghosts throw at people?

Boo-merangs.

How did the teacher grow his jacket? In the elbow patch

Q. Why is the coffee always lonely?

A. Because all the tea leaves.

How to massage People by Hans On

The good news is you're going to be a hit rapper this Xmas

The bad news is its in a department store

What sport always takes place in the garden? Fencing.

What kind of planes carry elephants?

Jumbo jets.

What do you have to look at longest to understand? The peeriodic table

Bradley: Are you really winning two games in chess club?

Sally: I'm not sure I'll just double check

My schools so broke the principal brought in fat kids, just so someone would buy band candy.

Cats always have an alibi, they never go anywhere without their tail.

Knock Knock

Who's there?

Mickey

Mickey who?

Me key's broken, let me in

Q. Why did the frog have to go to work?

A. Because his car was toad.

What do donkeys use instead of a see-saw?

A hee-haw

How to panic by Fran Tic

When I went to school we learned all about the founding fathers

You went to school with the founding fathers dad

What do you call a clown opera?

A musicfool.

What rental company only lends to women?

Mavis motors.

I'm like an Olympic athlete, you only see me running 4 times a year.

My son is a whizz on the computer, he can find all sorts of confidential information. We're thinking of enrolling him in a Hackademy

Teacher: Do you think John needs homeschooling?

John's Mum: No I think John's house is clever enough already

Knock Knock

Who's there?

Paul

Paul who?

Pull the door open, it's cold out here!

Q. Why didn't the fuzzy Australian animal get into college?

A. He didn't have the KUALAfications.

Q. What's a dog's favorite part of a gold course?

A. The ruff!

How to keep your dog fit by Doc Walker

Knock knock

Who's there?

Lass

Lass who?

The cattle dummy

We had to dissect a frog in class today.

Do they still do that in chemistry?

It was a French lesson.

Waiter is this conspiracy stew?

Why do you ask?

It's hard to swallow.

What did the ghost do when his hair got to long?

He got a scare cut.

Pottery film

With Val Kilner

Mr and Mrs Thon and their athletic daughter Mary

My last holiday was all at sea

It was a cruise.

My Pet Chicken has just written his Autobiography. Next week he's having a 'Book Book Book' signing.

Q. Why wouldn't anyone believe the big cat?

A. Because he was always lion.

Why couldn't the girl stop playing hockey?

Hockey sticks

On giving up by Peter Out.

The cookery teacher was always stirring things up.

Knock knock

Who's there?

I'd kish

I'd kish who?

Then kiss me you fool!

How do you use twitter on a diet?

With artificial tweetners.

I'm flying to the capital of Norway?

Oslo?

No the jets quite fast.

I only steal boring, brown cars.

It's bland theft auto.

What singer hasn't got sleeves?

Kanye Vest.

What do all hippy cars come with?

Flower steering.

Q. How do patriots get through snow?

A. A Sledge of Allegiance

How does the bird get up high?

It s-wings

The good news is I found your rabbit

The bad news is the cat found it first

What pastas best for a diet? Lessen ya

My life in a petrol station by Phil M Up

Knock knock

Who's there?

Cash

Cash who?

Go away I have a nut allergy

I knew the English teacher was going to spell trouble.

Waiter how many people do your pies serve?

3.142 exactly.

What's ipad short for? I paid too much for an Apple.

Who haunts chicken farms?

Poultry geists

Mr and Mrs Fidel and their disapointing son Second.

When you said we were spending our holiday by the pool.

I didn't think we were going to a snooker hall!

A man robbed a shop with a colander today.

Police are looking for a shop sifter.

Who makes dam fine music? Justin Beaver.

What do you call a fat muscle car?

A Podge Mustang.

I keep people from Poland in my cellar; I hope to win the Pole vault.

I was going to invest in a meat by airmail company.

But the steaks were too high.

Who handles the mobile phones at the circus?

The ring master.

Why was coffee banned from the staff room? Because of all the tea-chers

If you learn maths you'll rule the world.

How?

Divide and conquer!

Q. Where do animals go to study the brain?

A. The Hippo Campus.

Q. How do you get fired from a job as a ski instructor?

A. Let your performance go downhill.

What should you do when you've watched too much television?

Televisioff

How to feel bad by Gill T Feeling

When I went to school we learned the differences between triangles

Only because you had to build the pyramids in gym class

Birds of the Antarctic by Penn Guinn

Knock knock

Who's there?

Tatt

Tatt who?

No thinks I'm too young.

God knows what the religious studies teacher was talking about.

Waiter is there clown in my lasagne?

Why do you ask?

It tastes funny.

If there's so many cats on facebook, why are our mice still attached to our computers?

What's got 4 legs howls at the moon and is nice to sit on?

A chair wolf.

Mr and Mrs Driver and their handy son Screw.

A man kidnapped 10 dogs yesterday, the police are following up leads.

Who's music is most infectious? Miley Virus.

Where do cars keep their lipstick?
In their clutch.

How do you greet a dinner lady? Jello!

Our school meat loafs so bad, it's meat coma.
I think the canteens serving rabbit meat in their hoppy joes.

Dad can I borrow your credit card?
Why?
We're studying biology.

Have you seen my Catfish? me neither so I don't know where he's getting those kippers from.

I said to the Apiarist. Do I have to pay for that one that just escaped? He said no, that one's a 'Free Bee'

Q. What's the heaviest type of rain?
A. Reindeer.

What kind of sandwich is always delighted? A thrilled cheese

When I was a boy we were so poor our baseball field had a zirconium
instead of a diamond.

How to read minds by Si Kick

Knock knock
Who's there?

See

See who?

But you only just got here.

Never date a tennis player; love means nothing to them.

When the circus sold it's lions

They lost their pride.

Why did the computer stop? Because of the key-bored

Our school sacked the head teacher, I think that shows a lack of principle.

My Cat now wants all his food boiled, Well that's a whole new Kettle of fish.

Q. Why was the buffalo procrastinating?

A. To bison time.

CPSIA information can be obtained
at www.ICGtesting.com
Printed in the USA
LVHW080352111222
734958LV00048B/2448